A REPORT TO CONGRESS

IN ACCORDANCE WITH §361(b)

OF THE

UNITING AND STRENGTHENING AMERICA BY PROVIDING

APPROPRIATE TOOLS REQUIRED TO INTERCEPT AND OBSTRUCT

TERRORISM ACT OF 2001

(USA PATRIOT ACT)

SUBMITTED BY THE
SECRETARY OF THE TREASURY

A REPORT TO CONGRESS
IN ACCORDANCE WITH §361(b) OF THE USA PATRIOT ACT

INDEX

EXHIBITS

A. FBAR Authorities under 31 U.S.C. 5314, 31 CFR 103.24, 103.32, 103.56, 103.57, and 103.59
B. Report of Foreign Bank and Financial Accounts (FBAR), TD F 90-22.1
C. Memorandum of Agreement and Delegation of Authority for Enforcement of FBAR Requirements, dated April 2, 2003.

I. INTRODUCTION

On October 26, 2001, the President signed into law the Uniting and Strengthening America by Providing Appropriate Tools Required to Intercept and Obstruct Terrorism ("USA PATRIOT Act") of 2001, Public Law 107-56. Section 361(b) of the Act provides:

> The Secretary of the Treasury shall study methods for improving compliance with the reporting requirements established in Section 5314 of Title 31, United States Code, and shall submit a report on such study to the Congress by the end of the 6-month period beginning on the date of the enactment of this Act and each 1-year period thereafter. The initial report shall include historical data on compliance with such reporting requirements.

The Secretary submitted the initial report in April 2002 and the subsequent report in the fall of 2003. In accordance with this requirement, the Secretary of the Treasury submits this third annual report.

II. BACKGROUND

The Bank Secrecy Act authorizes the Secretary of the Treasury to require reports and records that "have a high degree of usefulness in criminal, tax, or regulatory investigations or proceedings, or in the conduct of intelligence or counterintelligence activities, including analysis, to protect against international terrorism."[1] Under the Bank Secrecy Act, the Secretary requires a number of reports including the Foreign Bank and Financial Accounts Report ("FBAR").[2] That part of the Bank Secrecy Act, codified as 31 U.S.C., Section 5314, authorizes the Secretary to require residents or citizens of the United States, or a person in, and doing business in, the United States, to keep records and/or file reports concerning transactions with a foreign financial agency. This provision reflected congressional concern that foreign financial institutions located in jurisdictions with strict bank secrecy laws were being used to violate or evade domestic criminal, tax, and regulatory requirements.[3] Pursuant to this authority, the Secretary issued 31 C.F.R. 103.24, quoted in full in *Exhibit A*, which states in pertinent part:

> (a) Each person subject to the jurisdiction of the United States (except a foreign subsidiary of a U.S. person) having a financial interest in, or signature or other authority over, a bank, securities or other financial account in a foreign country shall report such relationship to the Commissioner of the Internal Revenue Service for each year in which such relationship exists, and shall provide such information as shall be specified in a reporting form....[4]

The form required by Section 103.24 is known as the Report of Foreign Bank and Financial Accounts ("FBAR"), TD F 90-22.1, the most recent version of which is attached as *Exhibit B*. Related records are also required under 31 C.F.R. 103.32.[5]

Once FBARs are posted to the Currency and Banking Retrieval System ("CBRS") financial database at the Internal Revenue Services' Detroit Computing Center ("DCC"), the forms are available for use "in criminal, tax, or regulatory investigations or proceedings, or in the conduct of intelligence or counterintelligence activities, including analysis, to protect against international terrorism."[6]

Administration of the Bank Secrecy Act, including enforcement, rests with the Secretary. The Secretary delegated this authority to FinCEN in 1994. Along with the IRS, examination

---

[1] See Titles I and II of Public Law 91-508, as amended, codified at 12 U.S.C. 1829b, 12 U.S.C. 1951-1959, 31 U.S.C. 5311 - 5314 and 5316 - 5332; and Title III, Sections 312, 313, 314, 326, and 352, Public Law 107-56, 115 Stat. 307.

[2] Regulations implementing Title II of the Bank Secrecy Act (codified at 31 U.S.C. 5311-5314 and 5316-5332) appear at 31 C.F.R. Part 103. The Secretary delegated the authority to administer Title II of the Bank Secrecy Act to the Director of the Financial Crimes Enforcement Network (FinCEN). By Memorandum of Agreement and Delegation of Authority for Enforcement of FBAR Requirements, dated April 8, 2003, FinCEN redelegated its enforcement authority to the Internal Revenue Service. This delegation is reflected in 31 C.F.R. 103.56(g).

[3] See *United States v. Clines*, 958 F. 2d 578, 581 (4th Cir.), *cert. denied*, 505 U.S. 1205 (1992).

[4] 31 U.S.C. 5314 and 31 C.F.R. 103.24 are included in Exhibit A.

[5] See Exhibit A.

[6] 31 U.S.C. 5311. The FBAR is not a tax return and is not to be attached to a taxpayer's Form 1040. Because an FBAR is a Title 31 report, it is not subject to the dissemination restrictions of 26 U.S.C. 6103.

authority for compliance with the Bank Secrecy Act was delegated to other agencies, such as the federal bank regulators. Civil examination authority for FBARs was included in Treasury Directive 15-41, dated December 1, 1992, which delegated to the IRS the authority to investigate numerous Bank Secrecy Act violations by nonbank financial institutions.[7] Civil violations were forwarded to the Treasury Department, and after 1994, to FinCEN, for consideration of whether to impose a penalty. Criminal examination authority for most Bank Secrecy Act provisions was delegated to IRS Criminal Investigation by Treasury Directive 15-42, dated January 21, 1999.[8] IRS Criminal Investigation ("CI") forwards cases that it recommends for prosecution through the IRS Office of Chief Counsel (which conducts its own independent review) to the Department of Justice, which has the final say on whether to initiate a criminal prosecution.

Under the Memorandum of Agreement and Delegation of Authority for Enforcement of FBAR Requirements dated April 2, 2003, FinCEN delegated all of its civil enforcement authority for FBARs to the Internal Revenue Service.[9] This delegation is reflected in 31 C.F.R. 103.56(g).[10] The delegation now allows Internal Revenue Service to create interpretive education outreach materials for the FBAR, revise the form and instructions, examine individuals and other entities, and assess civil penalties for violations.

III. PROGRESS ON OBJECTIVES

As a result of the study required under §361(b) of the USA PATRIOT Act, FinCEN articulated certain objectives in the first report issued in April 2002.

1. Delegation of Penalty Authority

The most far-reaching objective in the first report was the consideration of delegation of FBAR enforcement authority from FinCEN to the Internal Revenue Service. After considerable discussion between the agencies, which is detailed in the second report, it was determined that FinCEN would delegate all its FBAR civil enforcement powers to the Internal Revenue Service. The delegation was completed in April 2003 and it required the Internal Revenue Service to develop many new tools to administer the FBAR program. For example, a FBAR case tracking database has been developed to monitor FBAR cases. The new database is maintained at the Detroit Computing Center where all FBARs are filed and stored, including FBAR cases. Many of the figures used for this report were derived from this database.

A System of Records notice was published, as a proposed rule, in the Federal Register on April 30, 2004, and became final on January 18, 2005. The Internal Revenue Service developed examination technique guides and field procedures and also provided training to all its examiners in a nationwide Interactive Video Training Class in July 2003. In addition, forms for the procedures were developed and prepared. These forms included:

---

[7] 31 C.F.R. 103.56(b)(8) incorporates much of this delegation.

[8] 31 C.F.R. 103.56(c)(2) incorporates much of this delegation.

[9] The Memorandum of Agreement and Delegation of Authority for Enforcement of FBAR Requirements is included in Exhibit C.

[10] 31 C.F.R. 103.56(g) is included in Exhibit A.

- Form 13535, Foreign Bank and Financial Accounts Report Related Statute Memorandum, required to be able to use information acquired during a tax examination in a related FBAR examination;
- Form 13536, Foreign Bank and Financial Accounts Report Monitoring Document, forwarded to the FBAR database at DCC for monitoring purposes;
- FBAR Warning Letter, Letter 3800, for use when the FBAR examination revealed a violation not warranting a penalty;
- Letter 3709, advising the addressee that penalties are proposed and including Form 13449;
- Form 13449, Agreement to Assessment and Collection of Penalties under 31 U.S.C. 5321(a)(5) and 5321(a)(6);
- Form 13448, Penalty Assessments Certification Summary (Title 31 "FBAR"), an internal use form documenting the date of assessment; and,
- Letter 3708, "FBAR Thirty Day Letter," Notice and Demand for Payment after Assessment.

To ensure consistent penalty application throughout the country, Internal Revenue Service developed guidelines for penalty assertion for use by examiners. Technical Services FBAR specialists were selected to provide ongoing technical support to the field. They received in-depth training at a meeting on FBAR issues in January 2004.

IRS SB/SE Counsel is reviewing all FBAR cases to ensure legal correctness in this first year. IRS SB/SE Counsel has appointed area counsel FBAR specialists to provide counsel a resource in this new field. Counsel broadcast an Interactive Video Training Class for all counsel on FBAR law and special procedures in January 2004 and a class for the IRS SB/SE Area counsel specialists later in the month.

The Anti-Money Laundering ("AML") team at the Internal Revenue Service, in addition to participating in all the above activities, has set up an FBAR website for internal use. This website contains much of the training material, as well as examination documents and FBAR Frequently Asked Questions.

2. *Update and Improve the FBAR Form and Instructions*

The first report stated that FinCEN would take responsibility for updating the FBAR Form, TD F 90-22.1, and the accompanying instructions. Comments received from filers indicated to FinCEN that an updated form should:

- eliminate duplication of information;
- incorporate user-friendly instructions;
- use understandable definitions;
- develop a continuation sheet for use by multiple filers;
- address procedures for joint accounts with spouses and business partners; and,
- include updated terminology and new types of financial transactions.

An updated form will assure that the form itself is not a barrier to compliance. FinCEN's target date to propose a revised form for public comment was no later than December 31, 2002.

In the second report, FinCEN stated that it had begun the process of updating the FBAR form and instructions to enhance the compliance of persons required to file this form. The target date of December 31, 2002, was extended.

With the delegation, IRS SB/SE accepted the responsibility of updating the form and instructions. IRS reviewed the electronic and hard copy files transferred by FinCEN in April 2003. These files included:

- An electronic folder of approximately 60 files containing FinCEN's responses to questions from the public regarding FBAR filing requirements from January 2002 to March 2003;
- An electronic copy of a draft revision of the FBAR and instructions dated March 7, 2003;
- A folder of various FBAR related materials provided by FinCEN which were selected for copying by Internal Revenue Service officials during their review, in the spring of 2003; and,
- Notes of materials provided for Internal Revenue Service review but not retention.

In addition to reviewing the FinCEN materials, the Internal Revenue Service used its own experiences in the 2003 FBAR filing season to determine areas causing confusion in completing the form. The Internal Revenue Service gathered information during the 2003 FBAR filing season respecting portions of the form that appeared to be causing confusion. This information included:

- A database of questions, created by IRS for this purpose, received from filers by AML Headquarters during the 2003 FBAR filing season;
- Questions and comments from IRS FBAR examiners; and,
- Questions submitted to the Detroit Computing Center from approximately 700 filers were received during the year. A list of Frequently Asked Questions was created and reviewed.

Finally, the Internal Revenue Service has adopted the same approach as FinCEN in concentrating on the instructions and leaving material revision of the form itself to another day.

Current draft instructions proposed by the Internal Revenue Service meet the following goals as outlined by FinCEN in the first report to the Congress:

- Eliminate duplication of information in the form;
- Incorporate user-friendly instructions;
- Use understandable definitions; and,
- Include updated terminology and new types of financial transactions.

Two goals that were not included in the draft instructions are:

- Develop a continuation sheet for use by multiple filers; and
- Address procedures for joint accounts with spouses and business partners.

These two goals are related because they anticipate that the form will change to allow one filing by multiple filers. The present form calls for only one filer per form. The Internal Revenue Service plans to specifically continue the present rule. This means, for example, that spousal filers of joint tax returns must nevertheless file separate FBARs if each has a financial interest in or signature or other authority over a foreign account. As there will not be multiple filers under the planned instructions, there is no need to develop a continuation sheet for use by multiple filers. The issue of permitting multiple filers needs considerably more study before adoption. Determined to meet the public's need for clarity, the Internal Revenue Service will study the multiple-filing issue for a subsequent revision.

Under the IRS' Multilingual Initiative, it has begun the process of translating the FBAR form and its instructions into Spanish.

3. Review Filing and Processing Procedures at the Detroit Computing Center

A third objective in the previous FBAR reports was to conduct a review of filing and processing procedures at the IRS DCC. This task was undertaken in 2003 by the Treasury Inspector General for Tax Administration ("TIGTA"). The TIGTA report entitled, "The Detroit Computing Center Adequately Processed Paper Bank Secrecy Act Documents, But Quality Reviews Should Be Implemented to Ensure Compliance With Quality Standards, March 2004, Reference Number: 2004-30-070" was published in 2004. The TIGTA audit of forms processing, including FBARs, by DCC found that "forms were timely processed to the CBRS database."

The IRS SB/SE Currency Transaction Reports Operations staff at DCC sorts FBAR materials by error type and sends correspondence on about 25 percent of the FBAR filings. About 75 percent reply to that correspondence. Based upon this information, the Internal Revenue Service can better determine what changes are needed on the form, as well as what outreach efforts might be appropriate. The staff also manages the new FBAR case tracking database. This database allows centralized tracking of FBAR cases which was previously not possible.

4. Evaluate Enhancing Outreach and Educational Guidance

Prior FBAR reports placed outreach and education as a prime objective. FinCEN did all outreach and education prior to the April 8, 2003 delegation to the Internal Revenue Service. The educational material was made available to the public via the FinCEN website. With the delegation, the Internal Revenue Service agreed to take responsibility for assessing whether better education and guidance regarding the requirements to file an FBAR was needed and, if so, to implement recommended improvements.

The IRS SB/SE Division is using its Taxpayer Education and Communication ("TEC") section to increase efficiency and standardize educational materials regarding FBAR compliance. TEC has developed a comprehensive marketing strategy that provides a framework for delivery of key messages, including identification of target audiences, identification of existing and alternative delivery channels and responsible parties. TEC's marketing strategy is designed to ensure broad based delivery of FBAR educational messages with the objective of encouraging voluntary filing and supporting compliance enforcement efforts.

TEC uses leveraged delivery channels wherever possible to ensure the widest distribution of materials through national and regional associations and organizations that the audience trusts and turns to for information. The campaign is built around this direct outreach effort that leverages relationships with outside stakeholders such as tax practitioner groups, financial associations, income tax software developers and the media. Direct outreach leveraged through outside stakeholders is the most economical and effective method to reach a diverse audience group. Leveraged delivery is a tool that allows us to work with third party organizations, including tax practitioners and financial associations that should be advising their clients to file the FBAR when appropriate.

TEC selected and trained six AML Specialists to deliver AML messages, including FBAR education. The TEC AML specialists gave 42 presentations relative to FBAR provisions to 4,120 tax practitioners and financial services providers between May 2003 and March 2004.

TEC is developing FBAR educational products to be used in direct outreach to deliver consistent messages relative to FBAR reporting provisions. These FBAR products include: a comprehensive PowerPoint presentation for use during outreach events; a Frequently Asked Questions sheet for dissemination to stakeholders; an educational news article created for dissemination to stakeholder associations for inclusion in their communication with their membership; a talking points document; and a "take-one" brochure.

The new "take-one" brochure, Publication 4261, "Do You Have a Foreign Bank Account," reminds foreign account holders of the reporting requirements. This publication is available on the IRS public web site at www.irs.gov/pub/irs-pdf/p4261.pdf and also will be available in tax practitioners' and brokers' offices as well as banks.

Under its Multilingual Initiative, the Internal Revenue Service has begun the process of translating into Spanish, Korean and Chinese FBAR outreach publications starting with Publication 4261.

Key messages included in the TEC AML products emphasize that enforcement has been delegated to the IRS by FinCEN, and that IRS is now investigating possible violations and will assess penalties, as appropriate. In addition, an overview of the law is included which covers the purpose of FBAR, reporting requirements, record keeping requirements, when and where to file, and information relative to penalties for failure to comply. Through research, TEC will develop measures to evaluate the effectiveness of the messages and the methods of outreach.

5. Establish Joint Task Force on FBAR Prosecutions/Enforcement

The first FBAR report mentioned the establishment of a Joint Task Force on FBAR Prosecutions and Enforcement. The second report recounted that this objective had "been attained in large part." Meetings were held between the IRS CI, Justice, Immigration and Customs Enforcement, and FinCEN in the latter part of 2002, as detailed in the second report. During 2003, continuing improvements in FBAR enforcement were made possible through a number of channels.

In January 2003, CI initiated an International Grand Jury to facilitate the investigation of individuals engaged in offshore tax evasion schemes. The basis for initiating the grand jury was the receipt of records of a foreign bank from foreign law enforcement officials. These records detailed the foreign bank's account information concerning approximately 550 U.S. taxpayers. Foreign law enforcement authorities have advised the CI International Attaché that the bank was used almost exclusively by individuals engaged in money laundering and related financial crimes. The records were provided to CI in an electronic format, and are being analyzed by the CI Philadelphia Lead Development Center. Analysis of the records indicates that some account holders have violated U.S. tax, Bank Secrecy Act (including FBAR), and money laundering laws.

The Internal Revenue Service is actively pursuing opportunities to share appropriate and legally permissible information between the civil and criminal functions. On a quarterly basis, representatives from CI and SB/SE meet to discuss coordination issues related to abusive offshore tax schemes. The CI-SB/SE Working Group was established in 2003 as a means for resolving issues related to the Offshore Credit Card Program ("OCCP"). The group has evolved to the point of handling all offshore compliance issues. The objective of the group is to share information, to improve communication between the operating divisions, and to enhance the shared processes, e.g., fraud referrals. By dealing with, and resolving, matters in the above manner, we are able to effectively manage the coordination issues related to our shared interest in offshore tax schemes. Information derived from the International Grand Jury (regarding approximately 550 bank clients) was provided in early 2004 to the civil side of the Internal Revenue Service with the understanding that the individuals will be evaluated for tax and FBAR compliance. Another example of this cooperative effort is an investment scheme where approximately 125 wealthy clients were identified by CI and turned over to SB/SE. A coordinated approach was used to identify the CI cases and transfer the remaining clients into SB/SE's hands for civil tax administration. The actions of all of these clients may result in potential FBAR investigations.

During the first four months of 2003, IRS sponsored an Offshore Voluntary Compliance Initiative under which the FBAR penalty was waived. It was followed by the Last Chance Compliance Initiative under which all but one year of FBAR penalties was waived. In 2003, the IRS Abusive Tax Avoidance Transactions ("ATAT") Offshore Transactions Initiative, including the Offshore Credit Card program, provided a productive vehicle for civil investigation of unreported FBARs. Internal Revenue Service's efforts to educate of all examiners involved in FBAR compliance has also resulted in a number of filings and penalties arising from general program examinations.

6. Results of IRS FBAR Enforcement on Compliance in 2003

Overall FBAR filings are increasing. During Calendar Year ("CY") 2000, a total of 174,528 FBARs were filed. By comparison, 204,689 FBARs were filed in CY 2003, a 17% increase over CY 2000. We believe the Offshore Initiatives have significantly contributed to this increase. For example, at the end of CY 2000, the Internal Revenue Service issued John Doe summons to the credit card companies, seeking information on their offshore account holders.

The Offshore Voluntary Compliance Initiative ("OVCI") required submission of delinquent FBARs. FBAR penalties were waived. The Internal Revenue Service received 1,299 applications from taxpayers for the OVCI. Once accepted, taxpayers had 150 days to submit complete packages including FBARs. OVCI records show that this initiative secured 2,099 delinquent FBARs.

The Last Chance Compliance Initiative, which also covered taxpayers using offshore credit cards, also required submission of delinquent FBARs to be considered in the program.

The Internal Revenue Service's FBAR enforcement actions have resulted in an increase in FBAR filings. Even though the offshore initiatives began in mid-2003, there have already been three civil penalty assessments totaling $148,567. Five FBAR cases were investigated and closed with no penalties during the CY 2003. In addition, multiple FBARs were secured. The ongoing offshore initiatives have already identified a significant number of potential FBAR cases and subsequent filings. During the decade preceding delegation to the Internal Revenue Service, only two cases were closed with FBAR penalties.

The results from CI show that the 2003 International Grand Jury resulted in five active criminal investigations. One of these has already resulted in a December 2003, forfeiture to the United States of $6,976,934.65 representing the illicit proceeds of an offshore internet gambling operation owned and operated from a foreign country by a target of the International Grand Jury. In addition to the five cases under active criminal investigation that have FBAR potential, 75 cases having FBAR potential were reviewed by the CI Philadelphia Lead Development Center. The review of cases from the 2003 International Grand Jury is ongoing. As of March 25, 2004, the results are: Negative/No Potential Cases – 37, In Process/Research – 10, Unassigned – 13, Referrals Sent to CI Field Offices - 15.

IV. CONCLUSION

Substantial progress has been made in the past year, particularly with respect to streamlining the administration and enforcement of the FBAR. In the coming year, the Internal Revenue Service intends to address the remaining tasks and continue making progress in our ongoing projects to improve compliance with the FBAR reporting requirement. Towards that end, the following specific goals have been set:

- Identify FBAR Non-Filers through enhanced examinations. This effort will focus first on offshore activities. The Internal Revenue Service will conduct reviews of offshore examinations with respect to the FBAR issue. An AML analyst has been assigned to review offshore examinations for FBAR issues in those locations judged to have the highest probability of FBAR violations. This review will focus on identification of FBAR violators and identification of barriers to such identification in the current examination process.

- Identify and correct any barriers to identification of FBAR violations existing in the current FBAR examination process. In particular, the Internal Revenue Service plans to create and deliver an FBAR training module for all incoming examiners. In addition, it plans to supplement the procedural memoranda that currently guide examiners with a new FBAR section of the Internal Revenue Manual ("IRM").

- Expand Outreach and Education to Potential FBAR Filers and Practitioners. TEC will expand outreach and educational efforts in 2004, based upon the results of initial activities. In addition, coordination with the IRS off-shore activities will be an area of emphasis to facilitate identification of targeted audiences. Outreach about the filing requirements of Section 103.24 will be reinforced with cogent, consistent messages relative to application of penalties for failure to meet the FBAR filing requirements.

- Issue an improved FBAR Form and instructions. IRS will work towards finalizing an improved FBAR and instructions to better enable taxpayers to comply with the law.

EXHIBIT A

FBAR AUTHORITIES

UNITED STATES CODE
TITLE 31 - MONEY AND FINANCE
SUBTITLE IV - MONEY
CHAPTER 53 - MONETARY TRANSACTIONS
SUBCHAPTER II - RECORDS AND REPORTS ON MONETARY INSTRUMENTS TRANSACTIONS

5314 Records and reports on foreign financial agency transactions. --

5314(a) Considering the need to avoid impeding or controlling the export or import of monetary instruments and the need to avoid burdening unreasonably a person making a transaction with a foreign financial agency, the Secretary of the Treasury shall require a resident or citizen of the United States or a person in, and doing business in, the United States, to keep records, file reports, or keep records and file reports, when the resident, citizen, or person makes a transaction or maintains a relation for any person with a foreign financial agency. The records and reports shall contain the following information in the way and to the extent the Secretary prescribes:

5314(a)(1) the identity and address of participants in a transaction or relationship.

5314(a)(2) the legal capacity in which a participant is acting.

5314(a)(3) the identity of real parties in interest.

5314(a)(4) a description of the transaction.

5314(b) The Secretary may prescribe --

5314(b)(1) a reasonable classification of persons subject to or exempt from a requirement under this section or a regulation under this section;

5314(b)(2) a foreign country to which a requirement or a regulation under this section applies if the Secretary decides applying the requirement or regulation to all foreign countries is unnecessary or undesirable;

5314(b)(3) the magnitude of transactions subject to a requirement or a regulation under this section;

5314(b)(4) the kind of transaction subject to or exempt from a requirement or a regulation under this section; and,

5314(b)(5) other matters the Secretary considers necessary to carry out this section or a regulation under this section.

5314(c) A person shall be required to disclose a record required to be kept under this section or under a regulation under this section only as required by law. [As added by P.L. 97-258, September 13, 1982.]

CHAPTER I
MONETARY OFFICES DEPARTMENT OF THE TREASURY

PART 103 -- FINANCIAL RECORDKEEPING AND REPORTING OF CURRENCY AND FOREIGN TRANSACTIONS

§103.24 Reports of foreign financial accounts.

(a) Each person subject to the jurisdiction of the United States (except a foreign subsidiary of a U.S. person) having a financial interest in, or signature or other authority over, a bank, securities or other financial account in a foreign country shall report such relationship to the Commissioner of the Internal Revenue for each year in which such relationship exists, and shall provide such information as shall be specified in a reporting form prescribed by the Secretary to be filed by such persons. Persons having a financial interest in 25 or more foreign financial accounts need only note that fact on the form. Such persons will be required to provide detailed information concerning each account when so requested by the Secretary or his delegate.

§103.27 Filing of reports.

(a)(1) A report required by §103.22(a) shall be filed by the financial institution within 15 days following the day on which the reportable transaction occurred.
(2) A report required by §103.22(g) shall be filed by the bank within 15 days after receiving a request for the report.
(3) A copy of each report filed pursuant to §103.22 shall be retained by the financial institution for a period of five years from the date of the report.
(4) All reports required to be filed by §103.22 shall be filed with the Commissioner of Internal Revenue, unless otherwise specified.
(b)(1) A report required by §103.23(a) shall be filed at the time of entry into the United States or at the time of departure, mailing or shipping from the United States, unless otherwise specified by the Commissioner of Customs.
(2) A report required by §103.23(b) shall be filed within 15 days after receipt of the currency or other monetary instruments.
(3) All reports required by §103.23 shall be filed with the Customs officer in charge at any port of entry or departure, or as otherwise specified by the Commissioner of Customs. Reports required by §103.23(a) for currency or other monetary instruments not physically accompanying a person entering or departing from the United States, may be filed by mail on or before the date of entry, departure, mailing or shipping. All reports required by §103.23(b) may also be filed by mail. Reports filed by mail shall be addressed to the Commissioner of Customs, Attention: Currency Transportation Reports, Washington, DC 20229.

(c) Reports required to be filed by §103.24 shall be filed with the Commissioner of Internal Revenue on or before June 30 of each calendar year with respect to foreign financial accounts exceeding $10,000 maintained during the previous calendar year.

(d) Reports required by §103.22, §103.23 or §103.24 shall be filed on forms prescribed by the Secretary. All information called for in such forms shall be furnished.

(e) Forms to be used in making the reports required by §§103.22 and 103.24 may be obtained from the Internal Revenue Service. Forms to be used in making the reports required by §103.23 may be obtained from the U.S. Customs Service.

§103.32 Records to be made and retained by persons having financial interests in foreign financial accounts.

Records of accounts required by §103.24 to be reported to the Commissioner of Internal Revenue shall be retained by each person having a financial interest in or signature or other authority over any such account. Such records shall contain the name in which each such account is maintained, the number or other designation of such account, the name and address of the foreign bank or other person with whom such account is maintained, the type of such account, and the maximum value of each such account during the reporting period. Such records shall be retained for a period of 5 years and shall be kept at all times available for inspection as authorized by law. In the computation of the period of 5 years, there shall be disregarded any period beginning with a date on which the taxpayer is indicted or information instituted on account of the filing of a false or fraudulent Federal income tax return or failing to file a Federal income tax return, and ending with the date on which final disposition is made of the criminal proceeding.

§103.56 Enforcement.

(a) Overall authority for enforcement and compliance, including coordination and direction of procedures and activities of all other agencies exercising delegated authority under this part, is delegated to the Assistant Secretary (Enforcement).

(b) Authority to examine institutions to determine compliance with the requirements of this part is delegated as follows: …

(8) To the Commissioner of Internal Revenue with respect to all financial institutions, except brokers or dealers in securities, futures commission merchants, introducing brokers in commodities, and commodity trading advisors, not currently examined by Federal bank supervisory agencies for soundness and safety;

c) Authority for investigating criminal violations of this part is delegated as follows: …

(2) To the Commissioner of Internal Revenue except with respect to §103.23.

(g) The authority to enforce the provisions of 31 U.S.C. 5314 and §§103.24 and 103.32 of this part has been redelegated from FinCEN to the Commissioner of Internal Revenue by means of a

Memorandum of Agreement between FinCEN and IRS. Such authority includes, with respect to 31 U.S.C. 5314 and §§103.24 and 103.32 of this part, the authority to: assess and collect civil penalties under 31 U.S.C. 5321 and 31 CFR 103.57; investigate possible civil violations of these provisions (in addition to the authority already provided at paragraph (c)(2)) of this section); employ the summons power of subpart F of part 103; issue administrative rulings under subpart G of part 103; and take any other action reasonably necessary for the enforcement of these and related provisions, including pursuit of injunctions.

§103.57 Civil Penalty.

(a) For any willful violation, committed on or before October 12, 1984, of any reporting requirement for financial institutions under this part or of any recordkeeping requirements of §103.22, the Secretary may assess upon any domestic financial institution, and upon any partner, director, officer, or employee thereof who willfully participates in the violation, a civil penalty not to exceed $1,000.

(b) For any willful violation committed after October 12, 1984 and before October 28, 1986, of any reporting requirement for financial institutions under this part or of the recordkeeping requirements of §103.32, the Secretary may assess upon any domestic financial institution, and upon any partner, director, officer, or employee thereof who willfully participates in the violation, a civil penalty not to exceed $10,000.

(c) For any willful violation of any recordkeeping requirement for financial institutions, except violations of §103.32, under this part, the Secretary may assess upon any domestic financial institution, and upon any partner, director, officer, or employee thereof who willfully participates in the violation, a civil penalty not to exceed $1,000.

(d) For any failure to file a report required under §103.23 or for filing such a report containing any material omission or misstatement, the Secretary may assess a civil penalty up to the amount of the currency or monetary instruments transported, mailed or shipped, less any amount forfeited under §103.58.

(e) For any willful violation of §103.63 committed after January 26, 1987, the Secretary may assess upon any person a civil penalty not to exceed the amount of coins and currency involved in the transaction with respect to which such penalty is imposed. The amount of any civil penalty assessed under this paragraph shall be reduced by the amount of any forfeiture to the United States in connection with the transaction for which the penalty was imposed.

(f) For any willful violation committed after October 27, 1986, of any reporting requirement for financial institutions under this part (except §103.24, §103.25 or §103.32), the Secretary may assess upon any domestic financial institution, and upon any partner, director, officer, or employee thereof who willfully participates in the violation, a civil penalty not to exceed the greater of the amount (not to exceed $100,000) involved in the transaction or $25,000.

(g) For any willful violation committed after October 27, 1986, of any requirement of §103.24, §103.25, or §103.32, the Secretary may assess upon any person, a civil penalty:

(1) In the case of a violation of §103.25 involving a transaction, a civil penalty not to exceed the greater of the amount (not to exceed $100,000) of the transaction, or $25,000; and

(2) In the case of a violation of §103.24 or §103.32 involving a failure to report the existence of an account or any identifying information required to be provided with respect to such account, a

civil penalty not to exceed the greater of the amount (not to exceed $100,000) equal to the balance in the account at the time of the violation, or $25,000.

(h) For each negligent violation of any requirement of this part, committed after October 27, 1986, the Secretary may assess upon any financial institution a civil penalty not to exceed $500.

§103.59 Criminal Penalty.

(a) Any person who willfully violates any provision of Title I of Pub. L. 91-508, or of this part authorized thereby may, upon conviction thereof, be fined not more than $1,000 or be imprisoned not more than 1 year, or both. Such person may in addition, if the violation is of any provision authorized by Title I of Pub. L. 91-508 and if the violation is committed in furtherance of the commission of any violation of Federal law punishable by imprisonment for more than 1 year, be fined not more than $10,000 or be imprisoned not more than 5 years, or both.

(b) Any person who willfully violates any provision of Title II of Pub. L. 91-508, or of this part authorized thereby, may, upon conviction thereof, be fined not more than $250,000 or be imprisoned not more than 5 years, or both.

(c) Any person who willfully violates any provision of Title II of Pub. L. 91-508, or of this part authorized thereby, where the violation is either

(1) Committed while violating another law of the United States, or

(2) Committed as part of a pattern of any illegal activity involving more than $100,000 in any 12-month period, may, upon conviction thereof, be fined not more than $500,000 or be imprisoned not more than 10 years, or both.

(d) Any person who knowingly makes any false, fictitious or fraudulent statement or representation in any report required by this part may, upon conviction thereof, be fined not more than $10,000 or be imprisoned not more than 5 years, or both.

UNITED STATES CODE
TITLE 31 - MONEY AND FINANCE
SUBTITLE IV - MONEY
CHAPTER 53 - MONETARY TRANSACTIONS
SUBCHAPTER II - RECORDS AND REPORTS ON MONETARY INSTRUMENTS TRANSACTIONS

5314 Records and reports on foreign financial agency transactions. --

5314(a) Considering the need to avoid impeding or controlling the export or import of monetary instruments and the need to avoid burdening unreasonably a person making a transaction with a foreign financial agency, the Secretary of the Treasury shall require a resident or citizen of the United States or a person in, and doing business in, the United States, to keep records, file reports, or keep records and file reports, when the resident, citizen, or person makes a transaction or maintains a relation for any person with a foreign financial agency. The records and reports shall contain the following information in the way and to the extent the Secretary prescribes:

5314(a)(1) the identity and address of participants in a transaction or relationship.

5314(a)(2) the legal capacity in which a participant is acting.

5314(a)(3) the identity of real parties in interest.

5314(a)(4) a description of the transaction.

5314(b) The Secretary may prescribe --

5314(b)(1) a reasonable classification of persons subject to or exempt from a requirement under this section or a regulation under this section;

5314(b)(2) a foreign country to which a requirement or a regulation under this section applies if the Secretary decides applying the requirement or regulation to all foreign countries is unnecessary or undesirable;

5314(b)(3) the magnitude of transactions subject to a requirement or a regulation under this section;

5314(b)(4) the kind of transaction subject to or exempt from a requirement or a regulation under this section; and,

5314(b)(5) other matters the Secretary considers necessary to carry out this section or a regulation under this section.

5314(c) A person shall be required to disclose a record required to be kept under this section or under a regulation under this section only as required by law. [As added by P.L. 97-258, September 13, 1982.]

CHAPTER I
MONETARY OFFICES DEPARTMENT OF THE TREASURY

PART 103 -- FINANCIAL RECORDKEEPING AND REPORTING OF CURRENCY AND FOREIGN TRANSACTIONS

§103.24 Reports of foreign financial accounts.

(a) Each person subject to the jurisdiction of the United States (except a foreign subsidiary of a U.S. person) having a financial interest in, or signature or other authority over, a bank, securities or other financial account in a foreign country shall report such relationship to the Commissioner of the Internal Revenue for each year in which such relationship exists, and shall provide such information as shall be specified in a reporting form prescribed by the Secretary to be filed by such persons. Persons having a financial interest in 25 or more foreign financial accounts need only note that fact on the form. Such persons will be required to provide detailed information concerning each account when so requested by the Secretary or his delegate.

§103.27 Filing of reports.

(a)(1) A report required by §103.22(a) shall be filed by the financial institution within 15 days following the day on which the reportable transaction occurred.
(2) A report required by §103.22(g) shall be filed by the bank within 15 days after receiving a request for the report.
(3) A copy of each report filed pursuant to §103.22 shall be retained by the financial institution for a period of five years from the date of the report.
(4) All reports required to be filed by §103.22 shall be filed with the Commissioner of Internal Revenue, unless otherwise specified.
(b)(1) A report required by §103.23(a) shall be filed at the time of entry into the United States or at the time of departure, mailing or shipping from the United States, unless otherwise specified by the Commissioner of Customs.
(2) A report required by §103.23(b) shall be filed within 15 days after receipt of the currency or other monetary instruments.
(3) All reports required by §103.23 shall be filed with the Customs officer in charge at any port of entry or departure, or as otherwise specified by the Commissioner of Customs. Reports required by §103.23(a) for currency or other monetary instruments not physically accompanying a person entering or departing from the United States, may be filed by mail on or before the date of entry, departure, mailing or shipping. All reports required by §103.23(b) may also be filed by mail. Reports filed by mail shall be addressed to the Commissioner of Customs, Attention: Currency Transportation Reports, Washington, DC 20229.

(c) Reports required to be filed by §103.24 shall be filed with the Commissioner of Internal Revenue on or before June 30 of each calendar year with respect to foreign financial accounts exceeding $10,000 maintained during the previous calendar year.

(d) Reports required by §103.22, §103.23 or §103.24 shall be filed on forms prescribed by the Secretary. All information called for in such forms shall be furnished.

(e) Forms to be used in making the reports required by §§103.22 and 103.24 may be obtained from the Internal Revenue Service. Forms to be used in making the reports required by §103.23 may be obtained from the U.S. Customs Service.

§103.32 Records to be made and retained by persons having financial interests in foreign financial accounts.

Records of accounts required by §103.24 to be reported to the Commissioner of Internal Revenue shall be retained by each person having a financial interest in or signature or other authority over any such account. Such records shall contain the name in which each such account is maintained, the number or other designation of such account, the name and address of the foreign bank or other person with whom such account is maintained, the type of such account, and the maximum value of each such account during the reporting period. Such records shall be retained for a period of 5 years and shall be kept at all times available for inspection as authorized by law. In the computation of the period of 5 years, there shall be disregarded any period beginning with a date on which the taxpayer is indicted or information instituted on account of the filing of a false or fraudulent Federal income tax return or failing to file a Federal income tax return, and ending with the date on which final disposition is made of the criminal proceeding.

§103.56 Enforcement.

(a) Overall authority for enforcement and compliance, including coordination and direction of procedures and activities of all other agencies exercising delegated authority under this part, is delegated to the Assistant Secretary (Enforcement).

(b) Authority to examine institutions to determine compliance with the requirements of this part is delegated as follows: …

(8) To the Commissioner of Internal Revenue with respect to all financial institutions, except brokers or dealers in securities, futures commission merchants, introducing brokers in commodities, and commodity trading advisors, not currently examined by Federal bank supervisory agencies for soundness and safety;

c) Authority for investigating criminal violations of this part is delegated as follows: …

(2) To the Commissioner of Internal Revenue except with respect to §103.23.

(g) The authority to enforce the provisions of 31 U.S.C. 5314 and §§103.24 and 103.32 of this part has been redelegated from FinCEN to the Commissioner of Internal Revenue by means of a

Memorandum of Agreement between FinCEN and IRS. Such authority includes, with respect to 31 U.S.C. 5314 and §§103.24 and 103.32 of this part, the authority to: assess and collect civil penalties under 31 U.S.C. 5321 and 31 CFR 103.57; investigate possible civil violations of these provisions (in addition to the authority already provided at paragraph (c)(2)) of this section); employ the summons power of subpart F of part 103; issue administrative rulings under subpart G of part 103; and take any other action reasonably necessary for the enforcement of these and related provisions, including pursuit of injunctions.

§103.57 Civil penalty.

(a) For any willful violation, committed on or before October 12, 1984, of any reporting requirement for financial institutions under this part or of any recordkeeping requirements of §103.22, the Secretary may assess upon any domestic financial institution, and upon any partner, director, officer, or employee thereof who willfully participates in the violation, a civil penalty not to exceed $1,000.

(b) For any willful violation committed after October 12, 1984 and before October 28, 1986, of any reporting requirement for financial institutions under this part or of the recordkeeping requirements of §103.32, the Secretary may assess upon any domestic financial institution, and upon any partner, director, officer, or employee thereof who willfully participates in the violation, a civil penalty not to exceed $10,000.

(c) For any willful violation of any recordkeeping requirement for financial institutions, except violations of §103.32, under this part, the Secretary may assess upon any domestic financial institution, and upon any partner, director, officer, or employee thereof who willfully participates in the violation, a civil penalty not to exceed $1,000.

(d) For any failure to file a report required under §103.23 or for filing such a report containing any material omission or misstatement, the Secretary may assess a civil penalty up to the amount of the currency or monetary instruments transported, mailed or shipped, less any amount forfeited under §103.58.

(e) For any willful violation of §103.63 committed after January 26, 1987, the Secretary may assess upon any person a civil penalty not to exceed the amount of coins and currency involved in the transaction with respect to which such penalty is imposed. The amount of any civil penalty assessed under this paragraph shall be reduced by the amount of any forfeiture to the United States in connection with the transaction for which the penalty was imposed.

(f) For any willful violation committed after October 27, 1986, of any reporting requirement for financial institutions under this part (except §103.24, §103.25 or §103.32), the Secretary may assess upon any domestic financial institution, and upon any partner, director, officer, or employee thereof who willfully participates in the violation, a civil penalty not to exceed the greater of the amount (not to exceed $100,000) involved in the transaction or $25,000.

(g) For any willful violation committed after October 27, 1986, of any requirement of §103.24, §103.25, or §103.32, the Secretary may assess upon any person, a civil penalty:

(1) In the case of a violation of §103.25 involving a transaction, a civil penalty not to exceed the greater of the amount (not to exceed $100,000) of the transaction, or $25,000; and

(2) In the case of a violation of §103.24 or §103.32 involving a failure to report the existence of an account or any identifying information required to be provided with respect to such account, a

civil penalty not to exceed the greater of the amount (not to exceed $100,000) equal to the balance in the account at the time of the violation, or $25,000.

(h) For each negligent violation of any requirement of this part, committed after October 27, 1986, the Secretary may assess upon any financial institution a civil penalty not to exceed $500.

§103.59 Criminal Penalty.

(a) Any person who willfully violates any provision of Title I of Pub. L. 91-508, or of this part authorized thereby may, upon conviction thereof, be fined not more than $1,000 or be imprisoned not more than 1 year, or both. Such person may in addition, if the violation is of any provision authorized by Title I of Pub. L. 91-508 and if the violation is committed in furtherance of the commission of any violation of Federal law punishable by imprisonment for more than 1 year, be fined not more than $10,000 or be imprisoned not more than 5 years, or both.

(b) Any person who willfully violates any provision of Title II of Pub. L. 91-508, or of this part authorized thereby, may, upon conviction thereof, be fined not more than $250,000 or be imprisoned not more than 5 years, or both.

(c) Any person who willfully violates any provision of Title II of Pub. L. 91-508, or of this part authorized thereby, where the violation is either

(1) Committed while violating another law of the United States, or

(2) Committed as part of a pattern of any illegal activity involving more than $100,000 in any 12-month period, may, upon conviction thereof, be fined not more than $500,000 or be imprisoned not more than 10 years, or both.

(d) Any person who knowingly makes any false, fictitious or fraudulent statement or representation in any report required by this part may, upon conviction thereof, be fined not more than $10,000 or be imprisoned not more than 5 years, or both.

EXHIBIT B
FOREIGN BANK AND FINANCIAL ACCOUNTS REPORT
TD F 90-22.1

EXHIBIT C

MEMORANDUM OF AGREEMENT AND DELEGATION OF AUTHORITY FOR ENFORCEMENT OF FBAR REQUIREMENTS, DATED APRIL 2, 2003

www.ingramcontent.com/pod-product-compliance
Lightning Source LLC
Chambersburg PA
CBHW080810290526
45790CB00008B/3642